MW00938589

A Prayer For Our Children

KEITH L. MAGEE

Foreword by:
Ambassador Carol Moseley Braun

ISBN: 978-1-4834-1658-8 (sc)
ISBN: 978-1-4834-1657-1 (e)

Lulu Publishing Services rev. date: 08/15/2014

Dedication

~ the memories of ~
Thelma "Nan" Wise, 1915 – 1995
Samuel D. Proctor, 1927 – 1997
Alvie L. Magee, 1945 – 2006

~ the rhythm of ~
Robert "Doc" Johnson
Arthur W. Hughes
The *missing* Chibok Nigerian Girls

To the angel in the airport in Chicago
O'Hare, disguised as a stranger…

And, to all of the children that I see in
airports and everywhere I go…

Contents

Acknowledgements

Thanks to all who encouraged me to write and assisted along the way. I'm gratefully to Dr. Charleen Brantley for being my first reader. Thank you to Myami Smith and Austin Washington for their research and helping me to organize my thoughts.

Thank you to members of The Berachah Church for allowing me to serve as your pastor and for sharing me with the world. Thank you to the University of Birmingham, England for granting me a space to consider, research and write.

I owe an enormous amount of gratitude to Karen Pritzker for her encouragement and pushing me to go beyond my present state and into my destiny.

My father Alvin Magee was such a solid figure, and yet his departure left me with men to keep me grounded. I'm grateful to the Honorable Deval Patrick, Bishop Eddie Long, Bishop John Borders, Pastor John Hannah, Vernon Jordan, Peter Edelman, Edward Hale and Reuben Cannon.

Thank you to my mother, Dr. Barbara Reynolds, for the birthing rhythm of the heart. Thank you to the women who give place to me in your lives: Caroline Cracraft, Julia Stash, Marilyn Katz, Shirley Magee, Jackie Jenkins Scott, Marjorie Craig Benton, Sunny Fischer, Patricia Terry, Jackie Nelson and the Honorable Sheila Jackson Lee.

Thanks to all of my friends, especially my best friends: Lenny Lopez, Enrique Young, Rachel Randolph, Robin Wong, Freddie Burwell, Melvin Washington, Joseph Patton, Patti Keenan and Richard Clay; my spiritual children: Bruce and Melissa Wilson, Jordan Powers, Kevin Owens, and Rickenia Coplin; 'All my children': Ariell Wills, Pierre Bennett, Morgan Turner Cohen, Cameron Magee, Che Williams, Christian Day, Sharon White; NPHM Youth Council; and to my Brothers of Kappa Alpha Psi, especially Kenneth

Gladden, Bernard McClellan, Al Williams and Jermaine Myrie.

A very special thank you to the one who heard the voice of God to be my assistant and from that day has been so much more, Beverly Jackson. A sincere thank you to 'my' Sister Norma Estwick, for you are a friend that sticks closer than a sister. Gratitude and thanks to Anthony Ferguson for your fidelity and support. Enormous thanks to Marisa Ioppolo-Armanios who often meets me on the moon.

Thank you to the many folks at USAirways who make life comfortable for me, especially in Chicago: Theo Brown and Sophie Rose, and John McDonald, VP, Corporate Communications.

A special thank you to Ambassador Carol Moseley Braun for her support and willingness to propel you to look within this text.

Last, but certainly the most important of all, thank you to God for helping me to understand how to *give thanks* in the dark spaces because it makes dancing so much better in the sun.

Foreword

At this moment, our children are urgently in need of prayer. UNICEF reports that 22,000 children die daily due to poverty. They die quietly in some of the poorest villages on earth, far removed from the scrutiny and the conscience of the world. They die in our cities from violence and neglect. They suffer from conditions not of their causing. We cannot continue to ignore the consequences of our inaction.

Prayer is that Great super-connector to a prayer-answering God who specializes in changing impossible situations. Prayer from earth moves heaven above and surely we can agree that our children, whether they are in Africa, Asia or the United States need help beyond what our earthly doctrines, systems, affiliations and networks can provide.

Prayer works. Prayer delivers. Prayer liberates. And that is why I am happy to support Rev. Keith Magee's presentation of this book of prayers. It is a communication and a summons from heart to heart to unite us in faith that the dreams for our children to have healthy, safe and productive lives can come true in our lifetime through our heartfelt petitions.

Rev. Keith Magee's heart is reflected in his tireless advocacy for a community of caring for the well-being of children. He consistently speaks with clarity as a champion for children, especially for the potential contributions they could make in turn if given the opportunity to develop to the maximum extent of their God given capacity. I have devoted much of my public career and private life in advocacy for the welfare of children around the world. I consider myself fortunate to have connected with Rev. Magee in his important work.

Rev. Magee and I share a common journey with dyslexia. If it had not been for prayer, and the caring and compassionate adults who could see beyond dyslexia's challenges, neither of us might have been able to help others. Today, children with dyslexia are seen as *living with a limitation*. Our own experiences convince us that they should be seen as capable of making tremendous contributions if a proper dyslexia diagnosis is used to tailor their education. We are working to ensure that their talents are developed and not overshadowed by that condition.

May our prayers affirm that with the help of God we can create a world in which all children are valued and our political, economic and social systems and institutions will begin to serve their interests, and not just the powerful among us. Prayer, coupled with works, can lift, edify, and bless us all. Your prayers and support of this effort can make a difference for the good of all children.

Ambassador Carol Moseley Braun

I pray, dear Lord, for our world

that it be changed for
our children's, children's children

– for Our Children

– Keith L. Magee

*"There can be no keener revelation of a society's
soul than the way in which it treats its children."*

– Nelson Mandela

Introduction

Several years ago, I began commuting between Boston, MA and Chicago, IL. One morning during my travels, as I was sitting in O'Hare International Airport, a woman next to me asked why I was beaming with such a glow so early in the morning. Surprised by her noticing, I said to her "have you seen the eyes, smiles, hair, clothing and brilliance of all the children about us?" I went on to tell her that I light up when I see children.

I have an abundance of hope in our children. As adults we have grown and evolved and I don't think that we are so conscious to admit that our hearts and minds have been framed by all that we've seen, heard and learned. The success of our future, the furtherance of mankind's possible world, that *looks* like what the Creator intended, lies within our children.

Our answer to a better world for all, is through letting go of the haunting memories of the past, while keeping the value of personal culture and yet understanding that each day we become new; renewed. Each waking opportunity we journey forward as we are moving towards a future that is whole. We must see that we are in a new place and time. A place that springs forth hope beyond anything that we can imagine, which has the intrinsic possibility for our children to exist in love and solidarity.

Our greatest assignment as community, elders, and parents is to pray for our children. Prayer is not something to check off right before bedtime or before a meal. Prayer is the core of our relationship with God and with each other.

I believe that God wants us to take on the responsibility of praying for and with our children. We should pray for them as we put them to bed and while they are asleep. We must let them hear us pray out loud, so that they know that we are talking to God on their behalf and are trusting God with their lives and future. We have the collective responsibility to let them know how much we love them and that loving other people, no matter what, is the greatest purpose for their lives.

It is my earnest hope that this collection of prayers, scriptures, quotes, meditations and liturgy will inspire us to pray and equip our children to be better. And, not just for our children but that this might be a seed for our children's children's children too.

Keith L. Magee
Birmingham, England

Faith & Hope

"When we see the face of a child, we think of the future. We think of their dreams about what they might become, and what they might accomplish."

– Archbishop Desmond Tutu

I pray for a world

where Faith is
an understanding of my belief
with respect for yours

– for Our Children

I pray for a world

that doesn't Erase the past
but writes on a new board
to celebrate a promise of the future

– for Our Children

A Prayer

I pray for a world

where the Hearts of Julius Rosenwald
and Booker T. Washington…
become the heartbeat of the land – again

where the Tenacity of Eleanor Roosevelt
and Mary McCloud Bethune…
becomes the strength of our hands – again

where the Insight of James Baldwin and
Robert Frost…
becomes the footprint of our minds – again

– for Our Children

For Our Children

"One does not become enlightened
by imagining figures of light, but by
making the darkness conscious."

– C.G. Jung

A Prayer

I pray for a world

where Consciousness that abounds
that is filled with enlightenment
where no darkness reigns

– for Our Children

For Our Children

I pray for a world

that creates the Thirst for
the Deposits of Azi Morton, Marian Wright
Edelman and Jackie Jenkins–Scott
the Generous gift of Barbara Hostetter,
Julia Stasch and Karen Pritzker
the Balanced accounts of Constance Baker
Motley, Sonia Sotomayor and Anne Burke

– for Our Children

7

"I simply can't build my hopes on a foundation
of confusion, misery and death…I think…
Peace and tranquility will return again."

– Anne Frank

I pray for a world

that understands
…the Crossing of the river of
Barbara Jordan
Vernon Jordan
Michael Jordan

– for Our Children

"Hope is the belief that destiny will not be
written for us, but by us, by the men and
women who are not content to settle for
the world as it is, who have the courage
to remake the world as it should be."

– President Barack Obama

Freedom

*"Freedom consists not in doing what we like,
but in having the right to do what we ought."*

– Pope John Paul II

I pray for a world

where King's Dream is confusing
to understand because we live

where the Table of personhood is spread
where the Content of character matters
where Freedom rings, rings, rings

– for Our Children

I pray for a world

where the Resilience of Helvécio Martins
– Awakens
where the Persistence of Sergey Izvekov
– Awares
where the Courage of Marie d'Youville
– Affirms

– for Our Children

I pray for a world

where an
Eye for eye
makes the world Blind

– for Our Children

For Our Children

"Therefore all things whatsoever ye would
that men should do to you, do ye even so to
them: for this is the law and the prophets."

– Matthew 7:12 (KJV)

I pray for a world

without "isms"
Race
Sex
Gender
…so that difference is valued and honored

– for Our Children

I pray for a world

where Happiness is really when
what you think,
what you say and
what you do
are in Harmony

– for Our Children

"I submit that an individual who breaks a law
that conscience tells him is unjust, and who
willingly accepts the penalty of imprisonment
in order to arouse the conscience of the
community over its injustice, is in reality
expressing the highest respect for the law."

– Martin Luther King Jr.

Safety & Protection

"In peace I will both lie down and sleep: for you alone, O Lord, make me dwell in safety."

– Psalm 4:8 (NAS)

A Prayer

I pray for a world

where our children never know unwanted
Hands
Touches
Looks

that the cycle forever be broken…
along with the Silence

– for Our Children

For Our Children

I pray for a world

that honors
Liberty as
Freedom as
Justice as
…for ALL

– for Our Children

"Keep your life free from love of money, and
be content with what you have, for he said,
'I will never leave you nor forsake you.'"

– Hebrews 13:5 (ESV)

Healing

"Then they cried to the LORD in their
trouble, and he saved them from their distress.
He sent forth his word and healed them;
he rescued them from the grave. Let them
give thanks to the LORD for his unfailing
love and his wonderful deeds for men."

– Psalm 107:19–21 (NIV)

I pray for a world

that knows
NO parkinson's
NO alzheimer's
NO diabetes'
NO aids'

– for Our Children

For Our Children

"Hate is too great a burden to bear. It injures
the hater more than it injures the hated."

– Coretta Scott King

I pray for a world

where
the "B" word means beautiful
the "G" is a gentleman
the "Ho" is a garden tool

– for Our Children

For Our Children

I pray for a world

where
t – Today's
h – Healers
u – Using
g – Gentleness

– for Our Children

A Prayer

"The weak can never forgive. Forgiveness
is the attribute of the strong."

– Mahatma Gandhi

Abundance & Joy

"Giving is the secret of abundance."

– Sivananda

A Prayer

I pray for a world

where poverty is of the past
and there is Plenty for the future…

Plenty of warm blankets and coats
Plenty of milk and bread
Plenty of water and green grass
Plenty of love and solidarity
Plently of laughter and joy

– for Our Children

For Our Children

I pray for a world

where
Amara of the Dingle's of Philadelphia
Nora of the Geuye's of Darkar
Chanel of the Armanios' of Perth

Share easy bake ovens

– for Our Children

I pray for a world

that doesn't
Build up
...but
Builds around

– for Our Children

For Our Children

I pray for a world

where
Alex Stromberg in Chicago
Curtis Rent in Pretoria
Vladimir Reznikov in Prague

Play soccer together on the same team –
in Caracas

– for Our Children

"To live a pure unselfish life, one
must count nothing as one's own
in the midst of abundance."

– Gautama Siddhartha

Inclusion

"*Exclusion isn't appropriate when prayers to a God who includes everyone in his love are being offered. Hindus, Sikhs, Christians, Muslims, Jews (to name a few) all have a different name for God, but it's the same God. Excluding a religion from a day of prayer just because it uses a different name for God misses the mark of recognizing that we are all children of God.*"

– Alex Howard

A Prayer

I pray for a world

where
Kinky hair and bright eyes
Oily hair and slanted eyes
Stringy hair and hazel eyes

can See
the me–in–me and smile as one

– for Our Children

I pray for a world

where God's love resounds
whether you're
Muslim
Shinto
Christian

when you're
Xo
Jewish
Buddhist

– for Our Children

I pray for a world

where language
represents diverse Sounds

where culture
represents new Ideas

– for Our Children

For Our Children

I pray for a world

that knows a
a black Prime Minister in England
a white Governor in DC
a hispanic Queen in Morocco
an asian President in America

– for Our Children

"Yes I am, I am also a Muslim, a
Christian, a Buddhist, and a Jew."

– Mahatma Gandhi

Family

*"What can you do to promote world peace?
Go home and love your family."*

– Mother Teresa

A Prayer

I pray for a world

where no parent fears their child's
Well-being

where police insure public safety
where priests pray, pray, pray

– for Our Children

For Our Children

I pray for a world

where Parents
understand that Listening is more
important than Speaking…sometimes

…because being Silent you can
Hear our Children

– for Our Children

I pray for a world

where Parents
understand that what you don't Know
can help you become better...

...because no one knows It All
and, being a great Navigator
is better than being a Dictator

– for Our Children

For Our Children

I pray for a world

of those
who's Wombs didn't hold
who's Seeds didn't plan

to multiple and release
more
nurturing, loving, giving, sharing

– for Our Children

"When you change a child's life, it's
not just that life. You start to change a
community, a family, and a nation."

– Oprah Winfrey

For Our Children

I pray for a world

where Mums cause their lads
to see that
Good can be
exchanged for
God

– for Our Children

A Prayer

I pray for a world

where every family's
Holes
are filled with the richest of
Wholeness

– for Our Children

"Let parents bequeath to their children
not riches, but the spirit of reverence."

– Plato

I pray for a world

that understands
blood maybe thicker
than Water

but Family is created
by those birthed out of Love
not blood

– for Our Children

Peace

"The lessons of the past can help to create a more promising future."

– Samuel Dewitt Proctor

A Prayer

I pray for a world

where the nobel peace prize doesn't exist

because we are all Helping others,
rather than ourselves

because we are all Pleasant,
without worries of harm

– for Our Children

For Our Children

I pray for a world

that knows no
Clinching of the pocketbook
Crossing to the other side of the street
Claiming of an innocent life

– for Our Children

"Peace I leave with you; My peace I give to you; not as the world gives do I give to you…"

– John 14:27 (KJV)

I pray for a world

where Peace…
Begins,
Middles
and
Ends
with Me…

– for Our Children

"Black Power is giving power to people who
have not had power to determine their destiny."

– Huey Newton

Charity

"When we give cheerfully and accept gratefully, everyone is blessed."

– Maya Angelou

I pray for a world

that believes in
Work above wealth
Enough above abundance
Giving above taking

– for Our Children

I pray for world

where waiting is Patience…
popcorn over an open fire
no cutting in line but valuing time

Time –
that moment, hour, day, year…

– for Our Children

A Prayer

I pray for a world

where
phd's are People Helper's Degrees
mba's are Mindful Brilliant Apprentices
rn's are Revered Nurtures

– for Our Children

For Our Children

"Mankind must remember that peace
is not God's gift to his creatures;
peace is our gift to each other."

– Elie Wiesel

A Prayer

"You will not attain righteousness till you
spend in charity of the things you love."

– The Qur'an, 3/92

Love

"When there is love, a cliff becomes a meadow."

– Ethiopian Proverb

I pray for a world

of shared love so
that a child in Liverpool can have a
beam in their eye

from how high they pushed the swing
of the child from Houston

that a child in Chicago can hear the laughter
because of the silly joke
of a child from Khartoum

– for Our Children

For Our Children

I pray for a world

that doesn't
know the meaning of
coon
spick
cracker
kayk

– for Our Children

A Prayer

I pray for a world

where…
beige
brown
slightly pink
reddish

Hands hold around the playground singing
Songs that spring up eternal love

– for Our Children

For Our Children

"Love has no awareness of merit or demerit;

it has no scale…
Love loves; this is its nature."

– Howard Thurman

Liturgy

This liturgy is an ecumenical source of praise and worship to the Creator. It serves as a prayerful action and symbol of the collective human spirit in reverence for our children. It is written across faiths with all children in mind. That we as adults might come to have clarity of heart, without regard of our individual faith, having simplicity in our concept that the Creator desires that we create a just world for our children. So as we gather in sacred spaces, community and in our home to pray for our children, let us be mindful that our prayers have the impact to change their future.

The liturgy is designed for the leader to serve as the reader. The leader as the reader must read with a passion to open the hearts of the hearers to understand that what we long for is a world that's better for our children. The leader as reader must make it clear that these affirmations, prayers and words are to cause us to atone, while presenting ourselves and our children before the presence of pureness.

For the respondent, they are to speak with authority, as a proclamation, that we pray this for our children. The sound of the collective voices should be audible, clear, and reverent, with faith and understanding. The power of our unity will cleanse and heal our world – for our children.

As you enter into this time of prayer begin with an opening as simple as:

We know that the Creator loves us
So let us pray for ourselves
And for others
We are one family
Filled with the same spirit of Love
So let us pray

– for Our Children

~ **Leader** ~

*"And he took a little child, and set him in
the midst of them: and taking him in his
arms, he said unto them, Whosoever shall
receive one of such little children in my name,
receiveth me: and whosoever receiveth me,
receiveth not me, but him that sent me."*

– Mark 9:36–37 (KJV)

~ **The People** ~

We pray for Our Children

*"There is no trust more sacred than the one
the world holds with children. There is no
duty more important than ensuring that
their rights are respected, that their welfare
is protected, that their lives are free from fear
and want and that they grow up in peace."*

– *Kofi A. Annan,*
The State of the World's Children 2000

~ The People ~

We pray for Our Children

~ Leader ~

"We reverently pray for eternal
harmony in the universe…
May the weather be seasonable
May the harvest be fruitful
May countries exist in harmony
May all people enjoy happiness."

— Buddhist Prayer

~ The People ~

We pray for Our Children

~ Leader ~

Children, obey your parents in the Lord: for this is right. Honor thy father and mother (which is the first commandment with promise), that it may be well with thee, and thou mayest live long on the earth. And, ye fathers, provoke not your children to wrath: but nurture them in the chastening and admonition of the Lord.

– Ephesians 6:1–4 (KJV)

~ The People ~

We pray for Our Children

~ Leader ~

O Thou kind Lord! These lovely children are
the handiwork of the fingers of Thy might
and the wondrous signs of Thy greatness.
O God! Protect these children, graciously
assist them to be educated and enable them
to render service to the world of humanity.
O God! These children are pearls, cause
them to be nurtured within the shell of Thy
loving–kindness. Thou art the Bountiful, the
All–Loving.

— *'Abdu'l–Bahá*

~ The People ~

We pray for Our Children

May God bless you and watch over you.
May God shine His face toward you
and show you favor.
May God look on you with favor
and grant you shalom peace.

– Numbers 6:22–27 (HET)

~ The People ~

We pray for Our Children

Lo, children are a heritage of Jehovah; [And] the fruit of the womb is [his] reward. As arrows in the hand of a mighty man, So are the children of youth. Happy is the man that hath his quiver full of them: They shall not be put to shame, When they speak with their enemies in the gate.

– Psalm 127:3–5 (KJV)

~ The People ~

We pray for Our Children

~ Leader ~

"We seek protection in the Perfect Words of
Allah from every devil and every beast, and
from every envious blameworthy eye."

– Al–Bukhari, 4/119

~ The People ~

We pray for Our Children

Let us know peace.
For as long as the moon shall rise,
For as long as the rivers shall flow,
For as long as the sun shall shine,
For as long as the grass shall grow,
Let us know peace.

– Cheyenne Prayer

~ **The People** ~

We pray for Our Children

Help us to keep our eyes fixed upon You.
Lord, be our richest treasure always.
You are our Healer, our Hope, and our
Strength. You are the God of miracles.
Work your miracles in our lives today and
keep changing us into your likeness.

– T.D. Jakes

~ The People ~

We pray for Our Children

And they were bringing unto him little children, that he should touch them: and the disciples rebuked them. But when Jesus saw it, he was moved with indignation, and said unto them, Suffer the little children to come unto me; forbid them not: for to such belong the kingdom of God. Verily I say unto you, Whosoever shall not receive the kingdom of God as a little child, he shall in no wise enter therein. And he took them in his arms, and blessed them, laying his hands upon them.

– Mark 10:13–16 (KJV)

~ The People ~

We pray for Our Children

~ Leader ~

God, I pray that we become a people that
can celebrate our alikeness that we might
be one. In our yielding state, that we realize
how blessed we are and that there are many
who don't have the opportunities that we
have; and knowing this we further commit
ourselves to the cause of equality and justice.

Cause us all to understand that difference is the
very thing that the You designed to bring us
closer together rather than further apart – We
pray this for our children's, children's, children.

– Keith L. Magee

~ ALL ~

We pray for Our Children – *And it is so…*

About the Author

Keith L. Magee, Th.D., FRSA, is a social justice scholar and pastor. He is a Distinguished Senior Fellow, University of Birmingham, England; Visiting Scholar, Boston University School of Theology; and Pastor, The Berachah Church, Boston, MA.

Magee is also the founding director of the National Public Housing Museum, Chicago, IL – having led its $12 million capital campaign.

Diagnosed with dyslexia, by a second grade teacher, he has personally taken on the charge of leading a diverse team to launch the Multicultural Initiative at Yale Center for Dyslexia and Creativity.

He is passionate about providing humanitarian aid to children and families. He is currently working with Harry Belafonte's on

Sankofa Project. He is the co-founder of Abba House, for children with HIV/AIDS in Abidjan, Ivory Coast.

He is a fellow of the Royal Society of Arts, United Kingdom. He is a member of the International Association for Religious Freedom, American Academy of Religion, Association for the Study of African American Life and History, and American Historical Association. He was honored to be inducted into the Morehouse College Martin Luther King Jr. Collegiums of Scholars and to serve as a patron of The CoED Foundation, United Kingdom. He serves on the board of advisors of the Anti-Defamation League-World of Difference Institute. He is also a life member of the Kappa Alpha Psi Fraternity, Inc.

Dr. Magee equally divides his time between the United States and United Kingdom.

For more information on Dr. Magee visit www.keithmagee.com.